HOT TOPICS

COSMETIC PROCEDURES

Geof Knight

Chicago, Illinois

www.heinemannraintree.com
Visit our website to find out
more information about
Heinemann-Raintree books.

To order:
☎ Phone 888-454-2279
📠 Visit www.heinemannraintree.com
to browse our catalog and order online.

Edited by Adam Miller, Andrew Farrow, and Adrian
Vigliano
Designed by Clare Webber and Steven Mead
Original illustrations © Capstone Global Library
Ltd.
Picture research by Ruth Blair
Production by Eirian Griffiths
Originated by Capstone Global Library Ltd.
Printed and bound in China by Leo Paper
Products Ltd.

15 14 13 12 11
10 9 8 7 6 5 4 3 2 1

**Library of Congress Cataloging-in-Publication
Data**
Knight, Geof (Geoffrey David)
  Cosmetic procedures / Geof Knight.
    p. cm.—(Hot topics)
  Includes bibliographical references and index.
  ISBN 978-1-4329-4868-9 (hc)
 1. Surgery, Plastic—Juvenile literature. I. Title.
  RD120.76.K65 2012
  617.9'5—dc22   2010046904

Acknowledgments
The author and publishers are grateful to the
following for permission to reproduce copyright
material: Alamy pp. **4** (© Allstar Picture Library),
13 (© Bernadette Delaney), **35** (© Peter Arnold,
Inc.), **43** left (© Pictorial Press Ltd), **45** (©
Wavebreak Media Ltd), **48** (© Chris Willson), **51**
(© Ray Evans); Corbis pp. **5** (© Jon McKee), **9**
(© Craig Tuttle/Design Pics), **22** (© Creasource),
27 (© Dennis Degnan), **30** (© Rainer Holz), **33**
(© Mike Watson Images Limited), **37** (© Eric
Cahan), **38** (© Fernando Leon/Retna/Retna Ltd),
40 (© Harry Briggs), **41** (© ERproductions Ltd/
Blend Images), **43** right (© Lorenzo Ciniglio), **46**
(© RCWW, Inc.); Getty Images p. **28**; Science
Photo Library pp. **14** (© PASCAL GOETGHELUCK),
21 (DR M.A. ANSARY); Shutterstock pp. **7**
(© EDHAR), **11** (© Ana Blazic), **16** (© Piotr
Marcinski); The Queen Victoria Hospital Museum
p. **18**.

Cover photograph of woman lying in hospital
bed, incision marks on her face reproduced with
permission of Getty Images (Monica Rodriguez).

Every effort has been made to contact copyright
holders of any material reproduced in this book.
Any omissions will be rectified in subsequent
printings if notice is given to the publisher.

CONTENTS

Some words are printed in bold, **like this**. You can find out what
they mean by looking in the glossary.

THE PURSUIT OF PERFECTION

Appearance can count for a lot. The first thing many people notice about each other is what they look like. Young people often worry about how others judge them, so making a good first impression can seem very important.

Major **media**, such as television, movies, and magazines, are full of images of people with perfect teeth, a perfect figure, a perfect tan, and more. Some people, especially young people, see these images and ask themselves some questions. Should they do something to change themselves—ranging from teeth whitening to tanning to plastic surgery—if it means fitting this ideal?

Some people have come to see **cosmetic** procedures, meaning procedures done to improve a person's appearance, as an accepted part of modern life. They argue that it is good for people's self-esteem to be able to change things they don't like about themselves. Others, however, believe that human beings should accept the appearance they were born with, grow with, and age with.

Two celebrities named Heidi have two different viewpoints about this issue.

Heidi Montag: Buying improvement

Heidi Montag, born in 1986, starred on the U.S. television series *The Hills*. In 2007 she had **breast augmentation**, **collagen** lip injections, and **rhinoplasty** (a "nose job"). Then on one day in November 2009, Montag had 10 more procedures.

■ Heidi Montag may not be satisfied...

Does this sound like obsession? Actually, Montag herself agrees! "I'm beyond obsessed," Montag said in January 2010. After her surgeries, she said: "It was so worth it! I see an upgraded version of me. It's a new face and it's a new energy … I'm very excited for the world to see the new me, and a real me."

By January 2010, Montag decided she wanted another breast augmentation. "I'm just starting," she said. "As you get older … there's a lot of maintenance. Nobody ages perfectly, so I plan to keep using surgery to make me as perfect as I can be."

Heidi Klum: Trusting nature

Heidi Klum, born in 1973, is a German–American model, television host, and producer. She has a very different attitude than Montag about cosmetic surgery. Klum has said: "I see that I've aged already. When I look at pictures now and when I see old pictures of me, of course I have aged. I don't think I would have plastic surgery. I'll be the only dinosaur in town, the only one that can actually move her forehead!"

Klum was included in the "Most Beautiful People" issue of *People*, a celebrity magazine, in spring 2009. At age 36, she agreed to be photographed without any makeup! The whole world could see her freckles, natural skin imperfections, and even a few wrinkles. Klum was praised by one writer for having "the courage to be shown looking like her real self."

■ …but Heidi Klum is.

What do you think?

What do you think about the viewpoints of the two Heidis? Are there aspects of each argument that you agree or disagree with? Why?

"Beauty is skin deep"

But is appearance everything? No doubt you have heard the phrase "beauty is skin deep." Corny? Sure. But it expresses the idea that someone's appearance may tell little about that person's character, personality, or intelligence. Many people would argue that all these things are far more important than appearance. When many people seek out friends or partners, qualities like character often count more than appearance. Moreover, even if looks attract people to begin with, if a good-looking person is not interesting or kind, people's interest will fade.

Many people disagree with society's increasing focus on physical perfection. And who can say what is "perfect"? Everyone has different ideas of beauty (see box below).

A new you?

This book will talk about the different ways—and reasons—people change their appearance. The most obvious ways are through things like dental treatments, makeup, cutting and styling hair, tanning, and piercing. But people also change their appearance through more dramatic methods. Doctors use surgical procedures that cut, reshape, and re-form the body and its parts.

WHAT IS ATTRACTIVENESS?

Why are some people thought to be attractive, while others are not? Certainly there are different standards of beauty throughout the world. But for most people, starting points are youth and health. Professional models chosen to sell fashions and products are usually young and healthy-looking.

However, people have different ideas about what makes a face attractive, whether it is eye color and eye shape, nose shape, hair color and style, skin color, or other factors. The same is true of body types. And these standards change over time.

As you read this book, think about your own standards of attractiveness. Do you feel that certain facial features or body types are more attractive than others? How do you think you developed these preferences? Were they affected by what you have seen in the media? Think also about how these preferences affect how you judge others—and yourself.

■ There are many ways to look attractive.

Are cosmetic procedures a good idea?

Some people think it is wrong for people to alter their bodies if physical health is not in danger. They think society places too much importance on appearance. But the issue is not always clear. What if people's self-esteem is very low because of their appearance? Or what if people's appearance or use of their body has been harmed by illness or an accident? Think about all sides of these issues as you read this book.

"Physical attractiveness creates a halo around a person..."

Psychologist Ken Siegel

EVERYDAY COSMETIC PROCEDURES

Not every cosmetic procedure involves doctors and surgeries. In fact, as part of our everyday life we try a variety of procedures to improve our appearance.

Teeth: The straight, white ideal

A person's mouth and teeth are central to appearance. The first thing that many people see is a person's smile, and we use our mouths to speak as well as to communicate.

For many cultures, crooked or yellow teeth are fairly common. But in the United States, straight, white teeth are increasingly viewed as normal. If people are not born with perfect teeth, they can get them through a variety of procedures and products. Because of the power of media in the United States, such as movies and television shows, this ideal of perfect teeth has started to change ideals worldwide about healthy and attractive teeth.

Are the perfectly straight, white teeth that are thought to be normal in the United States something that other countries should also copy? Or are imperfect teeth okay?

Orthodontia

Orthodontia, or braces, make crooked teeth straight. Braces take a long time to improve teeth—usually two years at minimum—and they are costly. They are very common in the United States and increasingly common in many places around the world.

Braces can improve people's confidence in their smile and whole face. But there are practical health reasons for braces, too. Crooked teeth make chewing more difficult. Because chewing is the first step of eating and digestion, teeth have to do their job right. Crooked teeth also can be more difficult to brush. This can lead to cavities.

Dental bleaching

Another common procedure is dental bleaching, also known as teeth whitening. When a dentist gives a patient a teeth-whitening treatment, results can last one or more years. But other types of bleaching are sold in drugstores and supermarkets, which makes them more convenient—although the results do not last as long. Because whitening treatments are increasingly affordable and easy to get, they have become wildly popular.

If people can have their teeth whitened every four to six months, will this make them more careless about caring for their teeth? Isn't there a reason to take good care of your teeth through a daily routine of brushing and flossing?

WARNINGS ABOUT TEETH WHITENING

While demand for teeth whitening is very high, dentists should be the ones to advise which option is ideal. Some people have very sensitive teeth. And home-use teeth whitening products can have side effects. They slightly reduce teeth enamel strength and, as a result, teeth can become even more sensitive. Teeth can also be overbleached (known among dentists as "over-white teeth"). However, these risks are small. For now, teeth whitening seems to be a procedure that will remain popular and trusted.

■ Brace yourself for straight teeth!

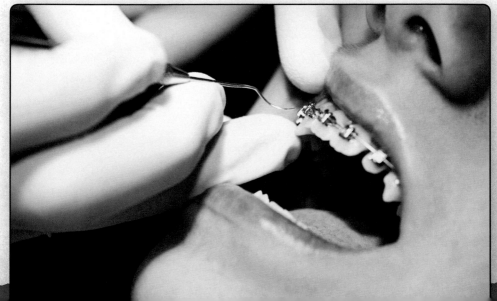

Makeup

For the past 5,000 years, women have used makeup to improve their appearance. Today, the U.S. cosmetics and beauty-aid industry totals over $20 billion in sales every year. Women buy basic products such as lipstick, concealer, and mascara to highlight their good features—and to downplay their bad ones. People also buy a variety of expensive creams and lotions that promise to get rid of concerns like dark circles under the eyes and wrinkles. In recent years, some men have also started to buy products such as concealer and wrinkle cream.

Although the use of makeup is widespread, it is criticized by some people, who say makeup is deceptive. What do you think? Is makeup "lying," or is it just presenting the best possible version of a person?

Hairstyles and body hair

The treatment of hair varies a lot by culture and age. As people get older, they might color their hair or try a variety of cuts and styles. But whereas hairstyles are seen as an expression of beauty, in many countries body hair is an entirely different matter. People go to great lengths to remove excess body hair.

Facial hair on men has varied throughout history (see box below). Currently, the majority of men in economically advanced countries usually shave facial hair. Some men remove chest and back hair as well.

THE MILITARY AND HAIR REMOVAL

From ancient times, the military has influenced men's hair removal. Alexander the Great, the ancient general, eventually insisted that all his soldiers shave. This was because many lost their advantage in battle when enemy soldiers grabbed their beards.

By the 19th century, facial hair was again common. But World War I (1914–18) changed that. To protect themselves from chemical weapons, soldiers needed to wear gas masks. By shaving their beards, they could seal a gas mask over their faces better. Since the public looked up to the military, most civilian men followed soldiers' "fashions."

Only in recent history have women removed armpit hair and leg hair (see box below). They also remove unwanted eyebrow and facial hair. **Depilation**—removing hair to skin level through the use of shaving or creams—is common. **Epilation**—removing hair entirely from the root—is popular, too. Done by tweezing or waxing, which can be painful, it lasts several weeks. According to a recent count, about 10,000 spas offered waxing for young girls and teenagers in the United States.

Do you think people need to go to all this trouble to remove hair? Isn't hair natural? Why remove it?

■ Girls commonly start using makeup when they are teens.

THE POWER OF TRENDS AND ADVERTISING

Until 1915, women in the United States and other Western countries generally did not remove underarm or leg hair. But new fashions emerged—dresses that were sleeveless, sheer, or had higher hemlines. They exposed arms and legs as never before. The razor company Gillette, wanting to increase sales, started to run ads in women's magazines mentioning how razors could remove "unsightly" and "unfeminine" hair. Within 20 years, hair removal and shaving aids for women were common. The custom—and advertising—continues today.

Piercing

You certainly know—or have already done—one of the simplest and oldest cosmetic procedures: ear piercing. It requires little time or money and is widespread.

Between 73 and 83 percent of women in the U.S. have their ears pierced. In addition, over 20 percent of men now get either one or both ears pierced. Other body parts besides ears are also now popular piercing points. Besides the ears the most common piercing points are the nose and belly button, but piercings are done on every body part imaginable. People get their ears pierced with piercing needles and piercing guns. Currently, most piercing is done by workers in shopping mall jewelry shops. But many piercing artists are against it. They say such workers are not trained enough in necessary **sterilization** (cleaning) techniques.

Pierced ears are so common that we may forget it is body alteration: it creates a hole in the skin! When you think about it, does it seem strange to do this just because other people do it?

LEGAL AGE AND RISKS

In the United States, if people under 18 want to get their ears pierced, most states require parents' permission. Should the age be younger? The risk to earlobes is very low, and they do not affect muscles, limbs, or internal organs. Contrast that with tongue or nose piercing. If not done safely, these piercings can be harmful. An improperly pierced tongue could affect speech. In the nose, the cartilage could be damaged, making breathing more difficult.

Tattoos

The choice to get a tattoo is one that should be carefully considered. Many people believe they look unprofessional, and a visible tattoo may mean that you lose out on your dream job one day. If you decide to get a tattoo, always research the studio to make sure it is hygienic. Diseases such as hepatitis B can be caught from needles. Also, remember that tattoos are difficult—even impossible—to remove. Tattooing a band's name on your arm when you're 18 may not seem like such a good idea 20 years later!

■ A girl undergoing the piercing gun.

DID YOU KNOW?

In India, nearly all girls and some boys get their ears pierced before they are five years old. Some are pierced as early as several days after birth. Similar customs are found in many South Asian countries.

Skin deep

Healthy and beautiful skin is considered an important part of attractiveness. Today, many people consider tanned skin to be an ideal. Tanning—and using tanning beds—is an increasingly common part of many people's routine cosmetic procedures.

THE STATUS OF TANNING

It is interesting that in Western countries, tanned skin was once looked down upon, while white skin was viewed as the most desirable and attractive. This was because tanned skin indicated that a person did outdoor work as a farmer or laborer—which indicated a lower social status. Today, with the majority of people working indoors, few people tan through their work. Getting a tan simply suggests an active, outdoor person, which are aspects that are generally viewed as desirable.

Tanning beds

Tanning beds have been around since the late 1970s. A tanning bed or booth is a device emitting **ultraviolet (UV) radiation**, like the rays of the Sun. People use this radiation to darken their skin, just as they use the Sun outdoors.

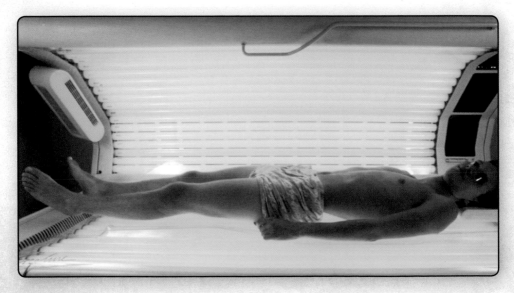

■ Healthy tanner, or future cancer victim?

A study released in May 2010 announced links between indoor tanning beds and **melanoma**, the worst type of skin cancer. Melanoma is the second-most common cancer in adolescents and young adults 15 to 29 years old. It is now known that people who use any type of tanning bed for any amount of time are 74 percent more likely to develop melanoma, and frequent users are two-and-a-half to three times more likely to develop it than people who never use tanning beds. Also, the risk increases over time.

Expert agencies such as the U.S. Food and Drug Administration (FDA) recommend that tanning beds should be avoided.

INTERNATIONAL RULES FOR SUN EXPOSURE

Some people wrongly think they need to protect themselves from the Sun's rays all the time. But the Sun is the only giver of vitamin D, which humans need to live. Rather, people should just be careful about how they expose themselves. The World Health Organization recommends the following rules for being in the Sun:

- limit time in the midday Sun
- seek shade
- wear protective clothing
- use sunscreen with at least 30 SPF
- avoid sunbeds (tanning beds)
- protect babies and young children: always keep babies in the shade

"Tanning beds are the cigarettes of our time: cancer-causing and poorly regulated."
U.S. congresswoman Carolyn Maloney

Healthy choices

If the popularity of tanning beds drops as a result of the study, it is possible that spray-on tanning will increase instead. The results of spray-on tans do not last as long as actually tanning the skin. But spray tans have no UV rays!

Given all this evidence, why do you think people would choose to use tanning beds? Would you choose your short-term appearance over your health?

WHY DO PEOPLE HAVE PLASTIC SURGERY?

Sometimes people go beyond everyday rituals like hair, makeup, or tanning to change their appearance. They decide to take the extreme step of surgery, which is often referred to as plastic surgery.

The number of people choosing to have plastic surgery has tripled since 1992. Perhaps even more extraordinary is the fact that the average age of patients expressing interest in having plastic surgery has fallen from 34 to 17 years old. What does this mean? Why would a teen want painful surgery with a painful recovery if there is no medical need for it?

The answers are complicated. But younger and mid-teens, particularly young women, often report having a poor body image. Teen interest in cosmetic procedures is overwhelmingly female. As girls become aware of their bodies and perceived attractiveness, outside images—like those in magazines and on billboards—provide ideals they want to copy.

■ Will this girl have plastic surgery?

Cosmetic procedures

For many people, plastic surgery is a choice made to look more attractive. These kinds of surgeries are called cosmetic procedures, and they include everything from breast augmentation to rhinoplasty to tummy tucks.

A CHOICE

Cosmetic surgery is usually not strictly necessary. So, it is also called **elective** surgery. People choose it to improve their appearance, not for health reasons or to function normally.

CASE STUDY

Evelyn

A 24-year-old, Evelyn, had a cosmetic procedure for appearance reasons. Evelyn said her breasts never developed during her teenage years. Her breasts then changed into what she described as "cone" breasts, and when she lost 16 kilograms (35 pounds), they sagged. She felt very embarrassed about them and "hated" her chest. Her best friend, who had had a breast augmentation procedure, recommended her plastic surgeon to Evelyn.

Evelyn had the procedure done and was happy with the results. She feels that her new breasts are natural-looking and beautiful. Evelyn says, "My plastic surgeon took all my hate towards [my body] away, and now has created high self esteem towards my body and esteem which I have not felt for a very long time."

WOMEN AND COSMETIC SURGERY

About 92 percent of cosmetic procedures over the last decade have been performed on women. Why do you think that is?

Reconstructive procedures

But sometimes people need to have plastic surgery to fix either **birth defects** or harm that has come to their bodies. Surgeries such as these are called **reconstructive** procedures.

THE GUINEA PIG CLUB

Some of the earliest patients for reconstructive surgery were injured pilots in the early days of World War II (1939–45). They had suffered horrible facial burns and injuries. Reconstructive surgery for such injuries was new and experimental. So, the injured pilots started calling themselves "The Guinea Pig Club" as a joke. But eventually, they actually did form an official group with that name!

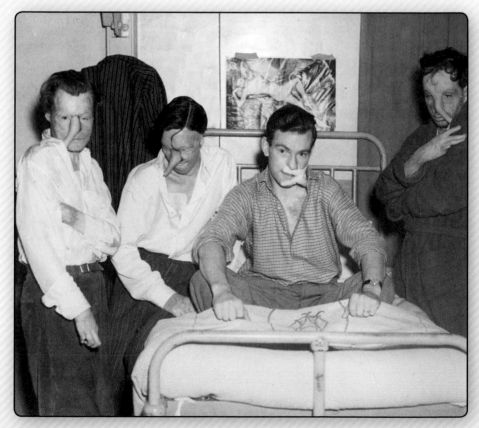

■ Some members of the Guinea Pig Club.

CASE STUDY

Kelsea Henderson

In 2008, 18-year-old Kelsea Henderson had her 17th surgical procedure. Since the age of 13, Kelsea had had many reconstructive surgeries to her back and chest. Kelsea needed the surgery because of the damage caused by a rare type of cancer located in her left chest, next to her heart and spinal column. It also surrounded nerves outside her spinal cord. Doctors started with traditional chemotherapy and radiation treatments to eliminate the cancer, but the treatments were not effective.

So, in April 2006, surgeons removed the cancer. To do so, they also removed portions of Kelsea's vertebrae and ribs, weakening her spine and chest. Where her ribs had been, the doctors put in artificial materials. To stabilize her spine, doctors inserted rods, screws, and bone grafts.

But over the next 18 months, a serious infection developed in Kelsea's rib area. Doctors removed the artificial material there and also materials used to stabilize her spine. The doctors transferred and re-attached parts of Kelsea's back and chest muscles, flaps of skin, blood vessels, and nerves.

For Kelsea's 17th and final operation in January 2008, the doctor took part of Kelsea's leg bone and placed it along her spinal column. A major leg vein was also moved to reestablish blood supply.

And just four months later, Kelsea attended her prom. She proudly displayed her scars, as they served as proof of all she had fought through.

Reasons for reconstructive surgery

Many people like Kelsea Henderson have reconstructive surgery to rebuild their bodies. There are three common reasons for reconstructive surgery.

Birth defects

Reconstructive surgery is necessary for birth defects. One example is a cleft lip and palate, which means the mouth's roof and top lip are badly shaped. A child with this problem cannot eat, breathe, or chew correctly. So, fixing it is truly practical and necessary—although the problems also greatly affect appearance.

Another birth defect is microtia. People with this condition cannot hear normally because of misshapen ears. A corrective procedure can greatly improve these people's quality of life.

What about people with ears that simply stick out a lot? Are such ears a birth defect, needing surgery? What do you think?

Burn victims

Reconstructive surgery is also necessary for severe burn victims. These victims often need **skin grafts**, meaning skin taken from another part of the body and placed on the injured area. Usually the graft is necessary for normal functioning and appearance.

PLASTIC SURGERY AND CONTROVERSY

Most people think reconstructive surgery is helpful and appropriate. But people disagree about cosmetic surgery, wondering how necessary and useful it is. Now that you have read some stories of people who have experienced both reconstructive and cosmetic surgeries, what do you think? Do both kinds of surgery help people? Or are they very different?

Breast cancer survivors

Breast cancer survivors also need reconstructive surgery. Breast cancer affects countless women each year, and for many, a **mastectomy**, meaning the removal of the breast, is necessary if the cancer is not caught in time. Each year more than 240,000 U.S. women are diagnosed with breast cancer and, on average, almost 25 percent of breast cancer survivors have reconstruction. Although some breast reconstruction is not strictly necessary to live, usually women who have had mastectomies need skin and tissue replacement in the chest area. Reconstructing breasts is a kind of finishing step in recovery.

All of these reconstructive procedures require money, time, and patience. But the people who have such procedures performed usually think they are well worth it.

INVASIVE AND NONINVASIVE

Cosmetic procedures are classified into a number of types. **Invasive** surgical procedures cut into the body. **Noninvasive** procedures do not cut into the body. Many skin-related cosmetic procedures are noninvasive or minimally invasive (see pages 22 and 23).

■ A child in need of cleft-palate surgery.

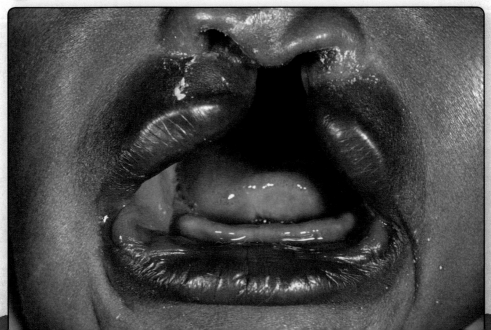

21

BUILDING A NEW YOU

A whole range of cosmetic procedures are available today, giving people the option to change anything from the shape of their calves to the number of lines in their forehead.

Noninvasive procedures

In recent years, noninvasive procedures that treat the skin have become increasingly popular. As they do not involve surgery or much recovery time, many people see these procedures as being a less-drastic alternative to surgery.

■ A woman getting botox injections.

Botox

Botox is a material used to "freeze," or paralyze, facial muscles, so that the skin does not show its natural aging wrinkles or sagging. It makes people look younger.

The popularity of Botox has exploded since it was approved in 2002 for use on wrinkles. From 2002 to 2009, the number of people getting Botox treatments increased 509 percent. As of 2007, it was the most common cosmetic procedure, with 4.8 million procedures in the United States alone. As seen with many cosmetic procedures, many more women than men get Botox injections—though the number of men having Botox procedures is on the rise. Despite the popularity, many people have worries about Botox.

CONCERNS ABOUT BOTOX

Botox's effects last for approximately 3–4 months. So, Botox is not a permanent procedure. This raises the possibility of **addiction**. Will people using Botox "need" to get injections 2–3 times a year in order to keep up their younger-looking appearance? Also, Botox has been criticized for making people look too smooth. People cannot move some muscles in their face, making them look like mannequins.

Other skin rejuvenation treatments

Botox is not the only skin **rejuvenation** treatment. Others are **dermabrasion**, **microdermabrasion**, and collagen injections. They are effective, but their results are not as long-lasting or wrinkle-free as Botox.

- Dermabrasion removes the top layers of the skin, smoothing the skin. It is helpful for facial scars, fine lines, and wrinkles. However, it takes two to three weeks to fully recover from the procedure.

- Microdermabrasion is another skin procedure. Tiny crystals are sprayed on the skin and cleaned off. It does not take as long as dermabrasion, but it is less effective. It works best on skin problems like fine lines, dull skin, brown spots, mild acne scars, and age spots.

- Another skin procedure is collagen injections. It is like Botox in that it is an injection. But collagen fills tissue, whereas Botox relaxes the muscles. Botox is used when lines appear with smiles or frowns. Collagen is used for always-present wrinkles.

WHAT DO YOU THINK?

At what age would you say these kinds of treatments are okay (if ever)? Or does age not matter—is it the number of wrinkles that matters? Do you think people should fight the aging process, or is it a natural and even beautiful part of life?

Breast augmentation

Many invasive procedures—which include all the risks of major surgery—are popular, too. For example, breast augmentation procedures are a very popular form of cosmetic surgery. In fact, breast augmentation is the most common surgical cosmetic procedure for women. (Botox is the most popular procedure of all, but it is not classified as surgery.) About 80 percent of breast **implants** are done for cosmetic reasons, while 20 percent are done for breast reconstruction after breast cancer surgery (see page 21).

Age and types of implants

Breast implants come in two types: **saline**, meaning saltwater, and **silicone**, a kind of gel. To receive saline implants, women must be 18. To receive silicone gel implants, women must be 22, because there are greater risks involved.

But it still may be unwise for young people to get implants, because young women's breasts continue developing into their late teens and early twenties. Also, young women may not be mature enough to make an informed decision about the potential risks (see page 36).

BREAST REDUCTION

Some women want breast reduction—the opposite of breast augmentation. Why do some women want breast reduction? Large breasts on a small body can be heavy to carry. This can cause sore shoulders and a sore back. Other women are made uncomfortable because of unwanted attention. So, for some women, breast reduction is a relief.

They will break!

Did you know that all breast implants eventually rupture if not replaced? Most implants last 7 to 12 years, but some break during the first few months or years. One manufacturer's own study found that between 3 and 20 percent of silicone gel implants break within 3 years.

If silicone gel implants break, it is usually what is called "silent rupture." This means women do not know when the implants break and leak. It may sound hard to believe, but only 30 percent of silicone gel implant ruptures are accurately diagnosed by medical exams.

Silent rupture is dangerous because it can lead to silicone migration. This is when the gel breaks down into liquid silicone, and this potentially damaging chemical then leaks away from the breast area. In one study, silicone migrated outside of the breast capsule in 21 percent of women. In those cases, it then migrated to lymph nodes and other organs. If this migration is not detected, it could even migrate to the lungs, liver, or other organs—which is even more damaging.

Other risks

There are other risks in breast augmentation. Some evidence shows that women with breast implants are at least three times as likely to not be able to make enough milk for breastfeeding if they have a baby. Other problems are hardening of the area, breast pain, and changes in nipple and breast sensation. The medical community is still researching these and other problems.

LEARN MORE ABOUT THE RISKS

Do research to learn more about the risks posed by breast implants. The following links are a good start:
www.breastimplantinfo.org/pdfs/JournalAdolescentHlth.pdf
and
www.breastimplantinfo.org/recon/implantfacts.html.

Do breast implants make women sick?

A controversial question is whether breast implants cause diseases or illnesses. The following are some problems that scientists have linked to breast implants. The evidence is not 100 percent proven, but the links are troubling.

Many studies suggest that implants affect the autoimmune system, which helps the body fight off illness. Autoimmune systems improved in 97 percent of the women who had their breast implants removed. Also, women with implants have been shown to be more likely to report fatigue (tiredness) and memory loss. Other diseases have also been linked with silicone implants.

Detecting breast cancer

Breast cancer is the most common cancer among women. Since tests called mammograms have been shown to detect breast cancer earlier and thus save lives, the question of whether implants interfere with mammograms is very important. It seems that they often do interfere. In fact, they can delay detection of breast cancer. Consider the following:

- Implants hide about 55 percent of breast tumors (masses of cells that can lead to cancer).

- Silicone or saline implants can rupture during mammograms.

- The bigger the implant is compared to a woman's natural breast size, the greater the chance there is for a less accurate mammogram.

WOOL BREASTS?

The history of breast implants shows how cosmetic surgery procedures have changed in terms of safety, testing, and standards. Procedures and materials improved because they had to improve. The earliest materials used for breast implants around 1900 were questionable ones: ivory, glass balls, ground rubber, ox cartilage, and wool! Silicone implants started to be used in 1961. But they were too hard, causing complaints that they did not feel real or lifelike. The next wave of implants in the 1970s felt more realistic. But too many leaked!

Memory and concentration

Women with implants have experienced memory loss, difficulties with concentration, and other brain problems. It is thought that the small amounts of platinum used to make silicone gel breast implants could be a cause.

Financial costs

As mentioned previously, breast implants eventually break. So, breast implant surgery is not a one-time cost. Because of the silent rupture risk, the U.S. Food and Drug Administration (FDA) recommends that women with silicone implants have an MRI (a kind of body scan) three years after the procedure, and every two years after that.

But breast MRIs usually cost at least $2,000. Moreover, cosmetic surgery is not covered by health insurance, and neither are the problems that may be caused by cosmetic surgery.

Despite these risks, thousands of women every year have the procedure done. Breast implants make many women feel good about their looks afterward. But anyone who is considering implants must think about the long-term effects of this choice.

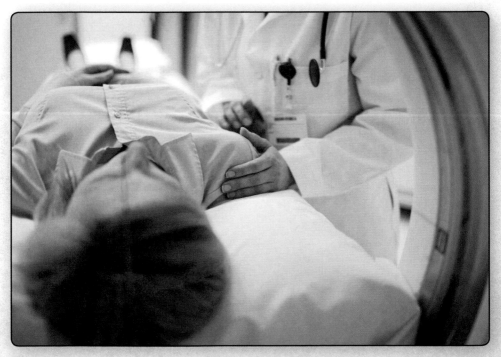

■ This woman is receiving an MRI scan. MRIs are able to produce images of the body's internal organs.

I need a lift!

Lifts are another popular cosmetic procedure. Lifts remove extra skin from the body. Extra skin can result when people lose a lot of weight. But most people have lifts to reduce the effects of aging: folding and sagging skin. In either case, people often worry about the unattractiveness of such skin. Lifts are a solution to remove the sagging and folds.

Face-lifts

Face-lifts are the most common type of cosmetic lift. Before the procedure, the surgeon and patient consult and draw the "cutting lines." Before the procedure, a patient is **anesthetized**. The surgeon then makes an **incision**, cutting from the hairline at the temples. Next, the surgeon cuts around the ear. The incision finishes in the lower scalp. The surgeon redistributes fat from the face, jowls, and neck, and underlying tissue is repositioned. Deeper layers of muscles are also lifted, while skin is reshaped and excess skin is trimmed away.

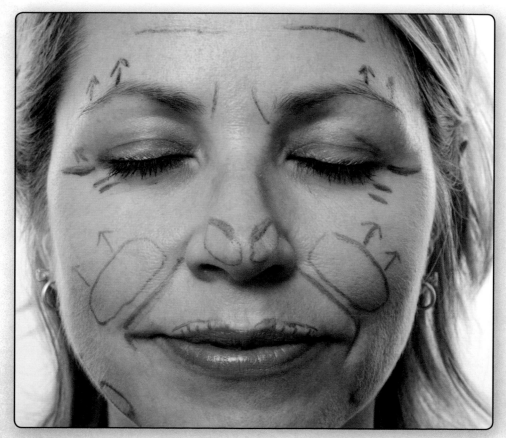

■ A woman whose face is marked for a face-lift.

Other lifts

Brow lifts are often performed together with a face-lift. They reduce the lines that develop across the forehead and improve what are known as "frown lines."

There are other types of lifts as well: breast lifts, thigh lifts, body lifts, neck lifts, and arm lifts. All lifts involve cutting and tightening the skin or smoothing fat. (Breast lifts differ from breast augmentation. A breast lift raises and firms the breasts by removing extra skin and tightening the tissue. Breast augmentation does not raise the breasts, but rather enlarges them.)

Risks and problems

Obviously, lifts are more complicated than piercing an ear or removing hair. Healing for face-lift patients is a bit of an ordeal—the body has just been cut and stitched up!

Patients have to wear a tight head wrapping for a few days and even a couple weeks, during which time they should not go anywhere. The face is swollen, bruised, and scarred from the incisions. Skin loss, numbness, discoloration, swelling, blood clots, and bleeding can also result. It may take several months for swelling to fully stop, and up to six months for incision lines to fade. These facts, and their impact on daily life, should be considered by someone thinking about a face-lift. Obviously, lifts can cause a lot of discomfort!

But despite all the possible trouble, many people think lifts are worth it. The popularity of lifts shows how people fear the effects of aging and wish to hide, eliminate, or reverse them. But aging is part of life. Should its effects be accepted? Or is it no big deal to get a procedure done to look younger?

LIFTS AND GENDER

Women have far more face-lifts than men. Why do you think this is? Does society have double standards for men and women in terms of showing signs of age? Will these double standards always be there, or can we change them?

"Who is this?"

Although cosmetic procedures remain popular, the spread of high-definition television—and with it, the audience's trained eye—has made it easier to spot a celebrity's bad cosmetic procedure. Few people in Hollywood are willing to admit to having most cosmetic procedures. But results are often painfully obvious and difficult to correct. Botox is a frequent enemy because the frozen muscles hinder making different facial expressions, which are as important to an actor as remembering script lines.

A casting director (a person who chooses performers for roles) said that when she was casting a movie in 2007, she received hundreds of head shots (pictures showing an actor or actress from the neck up). Some of the actresses who arrived for auditions, though, looked nothing like their photographs. Many of them had undergone cosmetic procedures to change their appearance.

"Behind the scenes, you have so many conversations," said a director, referring to his discussions with studio executives about actresses who had changed their looks through surgery. "'Why did she do that to herself? She was beautiful. She was great. But now we can't cast her.'"

Such recent standards can seem almost cruel. Youthful perfection is prized in Hollywood. But now many actors and actresses cannot get jobs, despite getting procedures.

■ A performer's looks are especially important when auditions draw hundreds of people.

Of course, there are still times when having cosmetic surgery can pay off. After many cosmetic procedures, Heidi Montag (see page 4) received a lot of media attention. She was soon hired for a movie and a television show. However, both parts poked fun at women who have had too much plastic surgery!

CASE STUDY

Changing Hollywood

In recent years, many Hollywood performers have used cosmetic procedures like Botox and breast augmentation to help them gain success. Now, those same procedures can sometimes prevent actors from getting hired!

In small but significant numbers, filmmakers and casting directors are beginning to re-think Hollywood's attitude toward breast implants, Botox, collagen-injected lips, and plastic surgery in general. Some television executives say they have begun casting more natural-looking actors from Australia and Britain because the performers at auditions in Los Angeles suffer from too much sameness. Their bodies are too perfect and they are often too young-looking.

Some casting directors are urging agents to discourage their clients from having surgery. A casting director said, "What I want to see is real." For example, moviemakers prefer actresses with natural breasts for historical dramas, which are set in a time before breast implants existed. When the Walt Disney Company advertised for extras in a *Pirates of the Caribbean* film, they specified that only actresses with real breasts need apply.

"The era of 'I look great because I did this to myself' has passed," said a director. "It is viewed as ridiculous. Ten years ago, actresses had the feeling that they had to get plastic surgery to get the part. Now … to walk into a casting session looking false hurts one's chances."

WHAT HAVE YOU GOT TO LOSE?

Weight loss procedures certainly relate to appearance, since they make a person slimmer. But they affect health, too, as the heart, other organs, and legs do not have to work as hard to carry weight.

Weight loss procedures fall into two categories. First, there are those that restrict the amount of food that the body processes—**gastric banding** and **gastric bypass**. Second, there are procedures that remove weight—**abdominoplasty** ("tummy tucks") and **liposuction**.

Gastric bypass

Gastric bypass surgery does not directly change appearance. The operation takes place inside the body. It changes the connection between the stomach and intestines. The stomach cannot absorb as much as it did before the bypass. People feel full more quickly than they did before the surgery. Thus, most people eat less, and they do not gain weight as easily as they used to. As a result, they get thinner.

But gastric bypass is not for everyone. It is mostly for those who suffer from an **obesity**-related disease that causes them to remain severely obese, even after trying to adjust their diet and exercise routines.

Gastric banding

Gastric banding places an adjustable silicone band around the upper stomach. Saltwater is regulated from a plastic tube connected just under the skin, which increases or decreases stomach capacity (the amount it can hold).

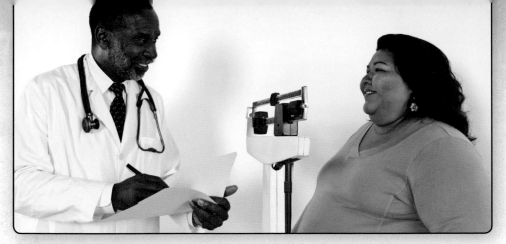

■ A weight-loss candidate discusses procedure options with her doctor.

Gastric banding has risks like nausea and vomiting. But these risks can be reduced by adjusting the band's tightness. Unlike gastric bypass surgery, gastric banding does not interfere with food being absorbed by the body. It could become more popular, since it is the safest weight loss procedure. The procedure can also be undone, and the stomach generally returns to its normal size. Gastric banding leads to the loss of about 40 percent of excess weight, on average.

Tummy tucks

Abdominoplasty, or a tummy tuck, removes excess fat and skin. People get a flatter, firmer stomach surface. It usually restores weakened or separated muscles, too. Also, unlike gastric banding or bypass, it does not limit the amount of food a person can eat. Tummy tucks do require weeks of healing time, though.

All of these weight loss procedures are helpful for some people. But they can be risky, just like any major surgery. There is a larger question, too: Could people who have these procedures lose weight by developing different personal habits, rather than taking the drastic step of surgery?

WHAT ABOUT SELF-CONTROL?

Weight loss procedures raise some questions: What's the point of self-control anymore? Could there be people who overeat and gain weight, thinking, "Well, I can just have a tummy tuck"? What is the value of eating a moderate-calorie diet and exercising instead?

Suck out the fat!

Liposuction is another weight loss procedure. The concept is surprisingly simple, but dramatic. The doctor cuts small incisions in the skin, then inserts a small stainless-steel tube into the fat. A powerful suction pump removes fat by creating tiny tunnels through the fatty layers. After surgery, these tiny tunnels collapse! As a result, the body is thinner.

Risks and limits

Like other procedures, liposuction is not risk-free. Healthy skin with good **elasticity** (stretchability) is essential. Why? Because after the fat is removed, when the skin "collapses," it must quickly adapt to the body's new shape and surface. Think of the skin as a rubber band that should be new, not old and stretched, for liposuction.

Liposuction has limitations. Less than 4.5 kilograms (10 pounds) of fat are removed at a time. But patients can still lose blood, and thus may need transfusions afterward. Ten pounds may sound like a lot, but not for the truly obese. Thus, doing liposuction over and over is not the safest or quickest way to lose weight. Liposuction is best for pockets of fat that are difficult to lose with diet and exercise—not for treating the entire body.

THE HISTORY OF LIPOSUCTION

Liposuction's history shows the importance of improving treatments after they are invented. Liposuction was first invented in 1974, and then further developed in 1978 in Europe. By 1980 liposuction was popular in the United States, but it began getting negative publicity. Patients experienced too much bleeding, and too many patients' skin had "ripples" or "dips" after surgery.

Then, in 1985, a U.S. **dermatologist** invented a technique for liposuction that eliminated the excessive bleeding and undesirable skin "ripples." Liposuction's popularity continued to grow. In fact, from 1998 through 2010 it was the most popular cosmetic surgical procedure in the United States!

Taking the easy way out?

Liposuction is convenient. But a healthy diet and regular exercise would remove the weight, too. So, liposuction raises a key question: Is dieting and exercise worth the "trouble"? Is it no big deal to just pay for the instant removal of weight?

Liposuction raises other questions. Many people have it done when they are not obese by any stretch of the imagination (or waistband)! When do you think weight loss procedures are okay?

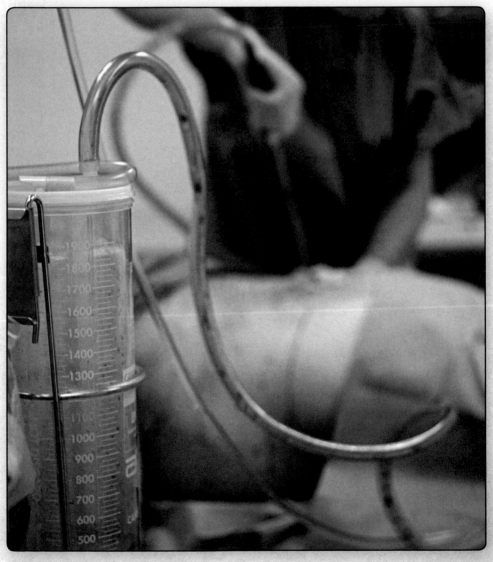

■ Fat being removed from a liposuction patient.

SELF-ACCEPTANCE– OR CHANGE?

As mentioned earlier, the average age of people interested in cosmetic procedures is going down all the time, with teenagers increasingly showing interest. More than one quarter of a million cosmetic procedures are performed on patients under age 19 every year. The majority of those are nonsurgical procedures such as laser hair removal and microdermabrasion. But surgical procedures like ear reshaping and nose jobs are also done.

Self-acceptance

Why do these young people feel the need to change themselves? As we have seen, young people sometimes suffer from low self-esteem, so they place a lot of value on how other people view them. The influence of the media causes many young people, especially young women, to feel that their own appearance does not measure up. But can these feelings be handled in a way other than cosmetic procedures?

WHEN IS SOMEONE READY?

Kids in Western countries must get parental consent for any surgical procedure if they are younger than 18. Both emotional maturity and physical maturity are issues. Is a teenager's body ready for a surgical procedure? As we have seen, patients must be at least 18 (sometimes older) for breast augmentation or liposuction. This is because the body has not finished growing.

Many experts recommend **psychiatric** evaluations for teens wanting cosmetic procedures. This will help ensure that they are making the decision for the right reasons. If you were a parent, when would you give permission for your teenager to have a cosmetic procedure?

The author Mark Twain once said, "The worst loneliness is not to be comfortable with yourself." Many people would similarly argue that learning to accept and value oneself is a huge part of growth. When people accept themselves, they do not feel overwhelmed by the need to gain other people's approval.

But such self-acceptance comes with time and maturity. If young people choose drastic cosmetic procedures, they might look back years later and regret that they changed who they were just to "fit in" (see pages 48 and 49).

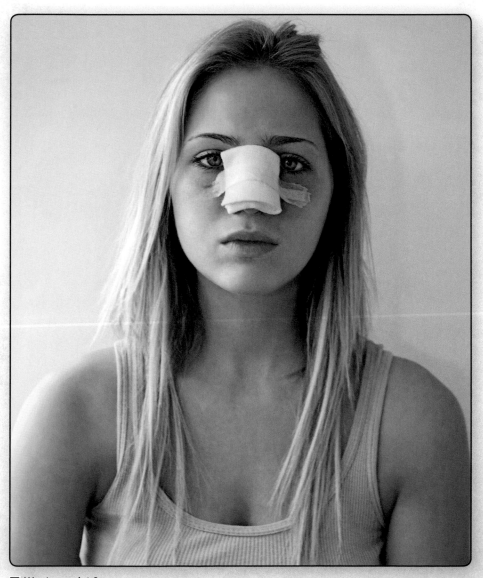

■ Was it worth it?

Should I change?

On the other hand, change is a part of life. An unknown author said, "Change is the essence of life. Be willing to surrender what you are for what you could become." That almost sounds like Heidi Montag (see page 4)! And the U.S. speaker Jim Rohn says, "If you don't like how things are, change it! You're not a tree."

Messages like these are also in the media and surrounding world, telling people that they can improve their grades at school, job performance, behavior—and their appearance. These messages suggest that people can empower themselves by taking control of their lives and their futures. Are cosmetic procedures just part of that thinking?

How much should people accept their appearance as it is? How much should they change it? Do you feel that certain changes—perhaps teeth whitening or Botox—are okay, but more drastic surgeries are not? Where do you draw the line?

■ Jocelyn Wildenstein has become known for having spent a huge amount of money on numerous cosmetic procedures.

CASE STUDY

Hooked on plastic surgery

One danger for people who embrace cosmetic procedures is that they can become addicted. In their pursuit of perfection, they are never happy and need to find more and more things to change.

This happened to a young Korean woman named Hang Mioku. Hang went to Japan in her twenties to have her first procedures performed. In Japan, they allowed her to have more surgeries than Korean doctors would allow. She liked the results and believed more operations would make her more attractive. But as she continued, her face became enlarged and deformed. Yet she still wanted more operations. The surgeons finally refused, however. One suggested psychiatric treatment.

When Hang returned to Korea, her own parents did not recognize her. Another doctor suggested psychiatric treatment. But instead Hang found a doctor who would perform silicone injections on her. Unbelievably, the doctor gave Hang her own syringe and silicone so that she could perform the injections herself. However, when she ran out of silicone, Hang switched to cooking oil! Her face became hideously huge.

Hang was featured on television. Viewers felt sorry for her and sent money to her to have operations to reduce the size of her face. A series of operations removed substances from her face and neck and reduced the swelling. But she was still scarred and deformed.

Even Hang can now understand the damage that she did. She now says that she would just like to have her original face back.

CASE STUDY

Western ideals in Asian culture

There is debate over whether or not it is healthy for people to change themselves with cosmetic procedures. Usually the debate is about whether or not it is okay to change an imperfect facial feature or body part. But what about when someone wants to change something fundamental about their cultural background?

For many years, European countries and the United States dominated not only economics and politics, but also popular culture throughout the world. Their stars and celebrities were worldwide ideals for attractiveness. As a result, ideals about attractiveness changed in Asia.

Asians are commonly born with a single eyelid. In contrast, Europeans and many Americans have "double eyelids," and so their eyes look rounder and bigger. For Asians influenced by Western media, Western eyes became a focus point: they look larger and are sometimes thought to be more attractive.

■ The eyes of Asian manga and anime characters demonstrate the ideal for eyes in Asian culture. Artists draw the characters' eyes as round and big.

CASE STUDY

"Western eyes"

Due to these trends, a "double eyelids" procedure was created and became popular in Asia. In this procedure, the skin around the eye is reshaped to create an upper eyelid with a crease. The resulting shape of the eyes is sometimes called "Western eyes."

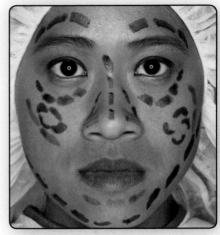

■ The number of Asian women having cosmetic procedures has increased a lot.

This is the most common cosmetic procedure in Taiwan and other parts of East Asia. Moreover, Asian patients usually are teenage girls, women in their early twenties, and men in their twenties or thirties.

Another recent development in Asia has been "circle lenses"—contact lenses that make the eye's iris (the colored part) and pupil (the central black area) look bigger. They are popular because they are cheaper, and less risky, than eye surgery.

Eyes are not the only feature many Asians are changing, however. They are increasingly asking surgeons for longer noses and fuller breasts—features not typical of many Asians.

But in recent decades, actors and actresses of Asian descent have gained an increased level of success in Hollywood and in world entertainment. Chow Yun-fat and Sandra Oh are two examples of such celebrities. Perhaps standards of attractiveness are changing, or widening. This could be related to the growth of the Internet, which spreads all different ideals—including Asian ones—around the world. All kinds of images of attractiveness are out there. Is it possible that there could be a reverse trend and "Asian eyes" could become the standard for attractive eyes before long?

RISKS, COSTS, AND REGRETS

When people decide to have cosmetic procedures, they must not take the decision lightly. They should do a lot of research to fully understand the risks, costs, and possible regrets involved.

Mistakes can happen

Just as in regular surgery, there is room for error in cosmetic procedures. These mistakes can be completely or mostly cosmetic. Ugly scarring often happens, requiring correction. But **botched** surgery can also harm tissue or body parts. Risks common among breast augmentation and face-lift patients are blood clots, infection, fluid accumulation, recurring pain, and poor wound healing.

Can it be corrected?

When botched procedures happen, patients often get angry, and some want justice. For example, in China alone, over 200,000 **lawsuits** were filed in the past decade against cosmetic surgery practitioners. In the United States, it is harder to get numbers. This is not the kind of information that the medical profession rushes to advertise!

PROCEDURES TO AVOID

There are procedures that even many cosmetic surgeons are against. Most agree that people should avoid lipodissolve, a shot that is supposed to dissolve away stubborn fat. Its chemicals have not been approved in the United States, and the treatment has often led to pain, swelling, hard lumps, and skin irregularities.

Most cosmetic surgeons also criticize cosmetic foot and leg-lengthening surgeries, both of which can cause long-term problems and pain.

"Revision surgeries" have also increased. These are surgeries required when the patient was not satisfied with the first surgery and wants it corrected. The demand for "revision surgeries" is so high some cosmetic surgeons now devote up to 50 percent of their practices to them.

■ The pop star Michael Jackson, seen here in his youth. His appearance changed dramatically over the course of his lifetime.

■ As an adult, Jackson admitted to having had nose jobs done. Many people think he may have been the victim of a botched surgery.

Trusting a doctor

To avoid botched procedures, it is absolutely essential to be sure that a doctor is **certified**. Being certified means that a doctor has been tested by other doctors to see if he or she meets requirements, such as passing courses of study and examinations.

Referrals are when patients tell other possible patients about their experience. These may also seem trustworthy, especially if they are from friends or relatives. But patients still must check the doctor's and clinic's certification and professional qualifications. Friends and relatives are still not experts and may not know enough about a surgeon's skill or success rate.

At what cost?

Americans spent almost $10.5 billion on cosmetic procedures in 2009—$6 billion was for invasive procedures, and $4.5 billion was for noninvasive procedures. By way of comparison, remember that the United States is the richest country in the world. It gives about $26 billion a year in foreign aid to other countries. That means that costs for plastic surgery are almost half that of U.S. foreign aid!

According to a survey, more people would have procedures performed if they had enough money! Moreover, most of the procedures they would choose would be invasive—the most difficult, time-consuming, and painful. In the survey, 29 percent of people said they would have a tummy tuck if affording it were not a problem, while 23 percent said they would have liposuction.

CASE STUDY

The personal costs of cosmetic surgery

About one-third of Americans who choose cosmetic surgery have middle-class or lower-class incomes. This means that procedures are not easily affordable for these patients.

Heidi Moore is someone who describes herself as a surgery and shopping addict. In 6 years Moore spent $100,000 on surgery, which contributed to going $200,000 in debt! She had an eye lift, two lip implants, a chin implant, her cheeks resculpted, liposuction on her neck, a tummy tuck, two breast augmentations, plus multiple Botox and laser treatments of wrinkles.

Moore got the money partly through identity theft—of her mother! She was able to juggle the debt from one credit card to another, but finally a detective caught her. Moore had therapy, but she would like one more surgery. She said: "I want my breasts made smaller. I hate them. I got them bigger so people would look at them, not me. Now I want people to see who I am."

Brain power and money, for what?

These and other figures show that in countries such as the United States, the United Kingdom, and many Asian countries, people spend a lot of money on cosmetic procedures. Not only money is spent, though. Resources such as time, human creativity, intelligence, and research capacity are also used. How many cosmetic procedure doctors and staff could possibly instead be researching how to treat and possibly even cure cancer?

Do you think research focused on cosmetic procedures could be better used for other human and global problems? Should societies be spending so much money, time, and research on cosmetic procedures?

■ What should doctors devote their talents to?

Cosmetic tourism

Cosmetic procedures have become so popular that they have led to "cosmetic tourism." This means that people go abroad and have cosmetic procedures done in countries where they are far cheaper, and where they can also enjoy a vacation! Cosmetic tourism website advertisements are powerful. The websites promise that everything is included and handled in one cost. They show attractive tourism spots like beaches.

Hundreds of thousands of Americans took such trips in the late 2000s. Some popular countries for cosmetic tourism are Thailand, Argentina, South Korea, Brazil, and the Czech Republic.

DID YOU KNOW?

Some people have trouble re-entering their home countries after a "cosmetic tour." Why? Because their passport photos are too different from their new, post-surgery face!

■ Some people are prepared to travel across the world for their cosmetic procedures.

Beware of aftercare

Cosmetic tourism is a serious matter, though, about which people need to be careful. For example, 25 percent of UK plastic surgeons reported they treated patients for problems relating to surgery done abroad (see box at left). Problems ranged from uneven breast augmentation to blood poisoning, blood clots, and wound infections.

This is not to suggest that all or most procedures abroad are bad. The American Medical Association does not discourage people from getting medical treatment abroad. There are qualified, certified doctors abroad, too. But patients have to be extra-careful and do research on doctors and clinics.

CASE STUDY

The story of Louise

A patient named Louise knows the risks of cosmetic tourism. Now in her forties, she had a botched nose job while on a trip to East Asia. The operation cost about $900. In her native United Kingdom, the cost would have been closer to $6,000.

Louise said this about her experience, "My nose was broken when I was a teenager and as I got older it became more prominent. I didn't plan [to have surgery at first], but was going on holiday anyway and a friend said they had the best surgeons in the world there and that it was cheap. So I went in to a center and was out in two hours. . . . But it began to smell funny and I went back a week later but was told it was okay."

The funny smell meant there was an infection. On returning home, she ignored the problem for four months before going to see her regular doctor. He applied repeated antibiotics, but they failed to work. By the time she saw a plastic surgeon in the United Kingdom, her nose had to be partially removed and eventually reconstructed. She has now had five operations to rebuild her nose because of the original infection that was not caught in time.

"I was too embarrassed to tell anyone what happened, other than my family. I told friends it was an injury. Even now they don't know the truth," she said.

Her doctor said, "Patients tend to leave [bad surgery] alone until it gets serious and then it requires more extensive treatment and even reconstructive surgery."

Regrets

Many people start to regret having their cosmetic procedures. Their regrets come not because of physical harm, but rather because their values and beliefs change, usually about themselves. Typical are the following comments: "I thought that I would like myself more"; "Implants did not change the way I felt about myself, it just made my clothes look better"; "I have come to realize that what's inside is what matters."

TATTOOING

Tattoos have grown in popularity through the last 30 years. Many people say tattooing is different from breast augmentations or face-lifts. What differences do you see? Does the fact that tattooing is "just on the skin" make it less risky than a procedure that "cuts"?

■ This person will die before the tattoos will.

Two nose jobs, two outcomes

Two girls' nose operations show how success and reactions can differ.

Patient A's story

"I decided to get a [nose job] after a successful breast augmentation with the same doctor. I can't imagine how much better it's going to look once the swelling goes down, which can take six months to two years. [It's] difficult to see yourself so beat up [as you recover], but after that clears up, you're fine. The packing [gauze pieces filling the nostrils] was the worst part, but I got mine removed the next day. Do your research—[get] tons of pictures from the doctors that [show] the progress of up to one year."

Patient B's story

"My nose was broken and I had to have work done on it. It was a disaster. They had to put an implant in my nose to build up the bridge (it was smashed). My body rejected it and I developed a bad infection that spread through my body ... it was life-threatening. They had an emergency surgery to take out the implant. I'm left with a very weird-looking nose. I've been researching good revision nose plastic surgeons. I know I have to ... have it fixed but I'm scared stiff."

Questions to ask oneself

Clearly, deciding to have a cosmetic procedure is a big personal and financial decision. Below are some questions people should ask themselves before making this decision:

- How long have I thought about this surgery?
- Why am I thinking about this surgery now?
- Are there other ways I can achieve the results I want?
- Am I expecting surgery to change my life as well as my appearance?
- Do I expect the surgery to improve my relationships?
- Am I getting cosmetic surgery to make myself happy or to please someone else?
- Can surgery really give me the look I want?
- Is this what I should be spending my money on?

People should ask these and similar questions, do a lot of research, talk to friends, family, and experts, and reflect before choosing cosmetic procedures. After all, the decision to have a cosmetic procedure is one that can stay with a person for life.

HOW TO FIND RELIABLE INFORMATION

Cosmetic procedures are big business. Because of that, **unethical** people can take advantage of eager, unwise people. It is important for people to get reliable information about realities and risks. They also need to find skilled professionals.

If people are interested in cosmetic surgery, it is wise to ask their local general doctor for information and recommendations. But these days, thanks (or no thanks) to the Internet, people often first try to educate themselves about procedures rather than consulting with experts. They also sometimes choose doctors directly from the Internet.

Are doctors salespeople?

How can patients find accurate and reliable information? A key point is to remember that much information out there—especially on the Internet—is from commercial organizations. They are trying to generate business, so they are usually **biased**. For example, a site that is connected to plastic surgeons might play down risks. So, people should check that a website is not a sales source for providers. They should try to find sites that provide information in a neutral way.

HUNTING FOR A BARGAIN?

Should a patient look for the best bargain? Saving money may be tempting. But hoping for the best work from the cheapest provider is risky, particularly in the case of overseas procedures (see pages 46 and 47).

Reliable resources

Websites that end with .org, .gov, and .edu are usually reliable choices. These sites are connected to or operated by educational institutions, the government, or other serious organizations. Making money is not their purpose, or at least not a primary one. Some reliable websites list doctors and hospitals that are certified and accredited (see pages 54 and 55). For information, a person should get at least two sources that are not connected. Seeing that a doctor has been certified by a credible professional organization is the best proof of all of a doctor's qualifications.

Online ratings

Some people also look at online service ratings. There, patients post comments about the quality of treatment and services. Patients' comments can be helpful. But they need to be examined very carefully, too. Is a review helpful and clear? Do the details sound sensible and fair? Or is the review wild and angry? Readers and prospective patients still must decide for themselves how worthwhile a review, or the provider it mentions, might be. In the end, sticking with local providers for information and services is the safest option.

■ It is essential that potential cosmetic surgery patients do their research before entering the doors of a clinic.

GLOSSARY

abdominoplasty also called a "tummy tuck," it is a procedure in which the stomach's skin is cut and then pulled, in order to tighten it

addiction being unable to resist something and feeling as though you "need" to do the activity or possess the thing

anesthetize to give a patient drugs and/or gases in an operation to relieve pain and alter consciousness

biased supporting one view only, often for reasons of gain

birth defect body feature that is irregular or abnormal at birth

botch to wreck, ruin, or make a mess of

Botox protein that is injected underneath skin in order to minimize or smooth out lines and wrinkles

breast augmentation increasing the size of breasts via silicone or saline implant procedures

certified checked and approved by the proper authorities

collagen protein that enhances elasticity and suppleness often used in skin substitutes

cosmetic having to do with appearance

depilation hair removal at the skin level

dermabrasion controlled scraping of the skin

dermatologist skin doctor

elasticity flexibility and stretchability. Skin with elasticity is necessary or helpful for many cosmetic procedures.

elective done by choice

epilation hair removal down to the root (below skin level)

gastric banding placement of a band around the stomach to reduce food intake

gastric bypass surgical reduction in size of the stomach

implant something placed and fixed inside something else. Breast implants are devices placed inside breasts to enlarge them.

incision cut into the skin

invasive type of procedure that requires doctors to cut into the skin or enter the organs of the body

lawsuit filing legal papers so that you can go to court to seek justice

liposuction procedure in which excess fat is removed by suction from under the skin

mastectomy procedure to remove a breast

media television, radio, publishing, and the Internet—the ways by which information and entertainment are packaged and sent

melanoma type of skin cancer in which the cells lose the ability to divide and grow normally

microdermabrasion more intensive under-the-skin procedure than dermabrasion which lasts longer

noninvasive type of procedure that does not require doctors to cut into the skin or enter the organs of the body

obesity condition of being grossly overweight

orthodontia straightening of teeth position and alignment

psychiatric related to the mind

reconstructive putting back together to a workable, near-original, or original condition

referral recommendation

rejuvenation regaining an original, stronger level of energy

rhinoplasty corrective surgery on the nose; sometimes called a "nose job"

saline salt-based substance or solution

silicone gelatin-based synthetic material

skin graft process of removing skin and attaching it to another area of the body; often done with burn victims

sterilization cleaning off germs and making something completely, clinically clean

ultraviolet (UV) radiation electromagnetic radiation; most UV radiation comes from sunlight

unethical not totally honest or honorable

FURTHER INFORMATION

Books

Campbell, Andrew. *Cosmetic Surgery*. Mankato, MN: Smart Apple Media, 2010.

Espejo, Roman. *The Culture of Beauty*. Detroit, MI: Greenhaven Press, 2009.

Libal, Autumn. *Can I Change the Way I Look?: A Teen's Guide to the Health Implications of Cosmetic Surgery, Makeovers, and Beyond*. Philadelphia, PA: Mason Crest Publishers, 2005.

Lustad, Marcia Amidon. *Cosmetic Surgery* (*Essential Viewpoints* series). Edina, MN: ABDO, 2010.

Websites

http://kidshealth.org/teen/your_mind/body_image/plastic_surgery.html
Kids' Health offers more helpful information about cosmetic procedures, written just for young people.

www.webmd.com
Visit Web MD and search on topics such as "cosmetic surgery" and "liposuction" to learn more about these topics.

www.womenshealth.gov/bodyimage/surgery/
This website of the U.S. Department of Health and Human Services offers advice for people considering cosmetic surgery, including whether they are good candidates for surgery and how they can find a reputable doctor.

www.hps.org/publicinformation/ate/faqs/tanningbooths.html
This website of the Health Physics Society offers answers to common questions about tanning.

https://extapps.ama-assn.org/doctorfinder/recaptcha.jsp

www.hospitalcompare.hhs.gov

www.abms.org

These websites list doctors and hospitals that are certified and accredited.

Topics for further research
- advertising and marketing beauty-related products
- anorexia
- body art
- exercise's effects on skin
- nutrition and diet's effects on appearance
- obesity
- skin care
- the cosmetic industry

Learn more about the risks
Do research to learn more about the risks posed by breast implants. The following links are a good start:
www.breastimplantinfo.org/pdfs, then click on:
   JournalAdolescentHlth.pdf
www.breastimplantinfo.org/reconimplantfacts.html.

INDEX